father cat:
STANLEY

mother cat:
SARAH

little brother cat:
GARY

baby sister cat:
PRISCILLA

Plate 1: **The Victorian Cat Family**

teatime

hot cocoa

fried chicken inside

picnic basket

hot tea

warm toast

mother's dressing gown
and hat

mother's picnic-time dress

small beaded bag

pretty picnic hat

hanky

afternoon dress

afternoon hat

brush   comb   mirror

Plate 2: **Mother's Clothes**

mother's best dress and hat

cat fan

mother's beaded bag

cat handkerchief

chemise

teddy bear—keeps baby quiet

mother's umbrella

tea tray with cat cookies

time for tea

mother's warm coat

mother's warm hat

Plate 3: **More of Mother's Clothing; Teatime**

father's hat

father's sailor hat

father's cane

father's nightcap

father's best suit

father's sailor suit

father's beach clothes

father's sleeping gown

Plate 4: **Father's Clothing**

father's warm hat

hat to wear to concert

father's warm winter coat

walking cane

time for hot cocoa

father's clock

cup of cocoa

father gives a concert

father's books on music and cat history

father's bathrobe

violin bow

soft pillow

father's cat violin

bowl of fruit

Plate 5: **Father's Belongings**

cup of milk

kitten bowl with warm mush

baby's bottle

baby's bib

toy clown

cut around dotted line

rompers

diaper

baby Priscilla goes out

warm suit and cap

sun hat

play dress

cut around dotted line

beach time

soft little pillow

baby's bow

toy bunny

party dress

sleepers

creeper

Plate 6: **Baby's Clothing**

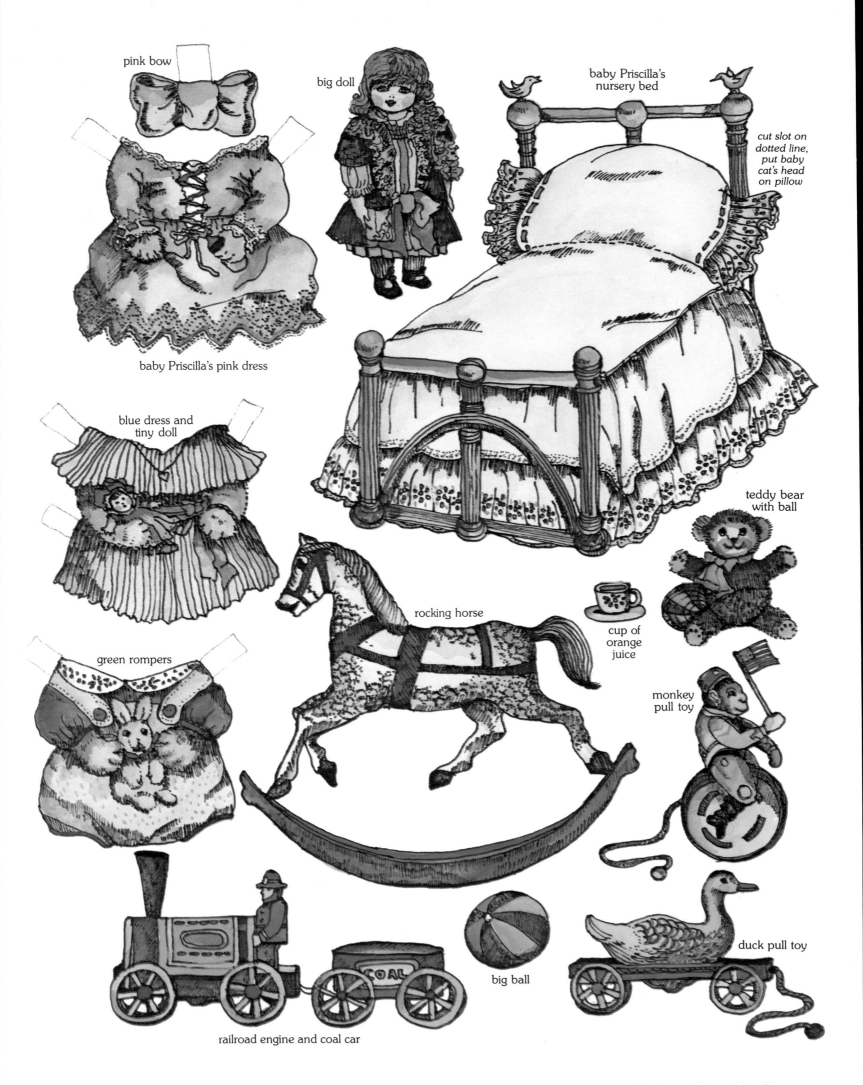

pink bow

big doll

baby Priscilla's
nursery bed

*cut slot on
dotted line,
put baby
cat's head
on pillow*

baby Priscilla's pink dress

blue dress and
tiny doll

teddy bear
with ball

green rompers

rocking horse

cup of
orange
juice

monkey
pull toy

duck pull toy

big ball

railroad engine and coal car

COAL

Plate 7: **Baby Priscilla in Her Nursery**

fishing hat

little Gary's dress clothes

hat

nightcap

suit

hot milk

fishing clothes

frog

apple

sleepers

fishing pole

fish

cap

ice-cream cone

beach ball

flowers

school clothes

sunsuit

lunch pail

shovel

school bag

towel

pail

garden clothes

baseball

cut on dotted line

bat

baseball cap

baseball uniform

blue bathrobe

milk and cookies

Plate 8: Little Brother Gary's Outfits

little Gary's train

circus truck

nap time

school outfit

cut hat on dotted line

play clothes and hat

dog Toby

boat

green tricycle

car with driver

ball

top

drum

horn

roly-poly

wind-up rooster and rabbit toy

blocks

safe

picnic outfit

bunny

Plate 9: **Little Brother Gary's Toys and Clothes**

fishing pole

father's hat

mother's hat

night owl

hiking clothes

big moth

father's camping clothes

hot cocoa

lantern

sharp hook—be careful!

baked beans

fishing creel

baby Priscilla's warm cap

baked potatoes and hot biscuits

cool cocoa

nice warm campfire

hot cocoa

baby ground squirrel

pillows and warm blankets

baby Priscilla's warm sleepers

little plump wild bunny

little Gary's boy-scout uniform

Plate 10: The Cat Family Goes Camping

dishes

napkins

bowls

spoons

party balloons

chocolate ice cream

Priscilla's new doll house

mother's party dress

new big blue bow

yellow hat

father has presents

party table and birthday cake

gifts

toys inside

little cat doll and her bottle

Priscilla's yellow party dress

cat baby buggy

brother Gary with present

bow came in this box

toy pig with clown

loud party horn

HAPPY CAT BIRTHDAY LITTLE PRICILLA!

Plate 11: **Baby Priscilla's Birthday Party**

sand

mother's beach hat

cat novel

little Gary's sailor hat

mother's bathing suit

beach umbrella

father's bathing suit

sand is everywhere

father's newspaper

mother's fan

nice picnic lunch

shovel

sand pail

pink lemonade in jug

cat doll

sailboat

her hat

beach ball

red bag

crab

Gary's bathing suit

big seashell

sand castle

Priscilla's bathing suit

toy duck

put on baby cat

starfish

beach towels

clam

fish in the ocean

sand

SUN TAN OIL

Plate 12: **The Cat Family at the Beach**

perching bird

cut on dotted lines in all hats

father's cap

pretty hat

binoculars for bird watching

thermos with iced tea

father's picnic clothes

mother's pretty picnic dress

yellow bow

picnic lunch

bananas

butterfly net

little butterfly

little red ants: Ned, Ted, Fred

big butterfly

sister's hat

brother's cap

brother's clothing

baby sister's picnic dress

mouse doll: Little Henry

ball

three apples

Plate 13: **The Cat Family Goes on a Picnic**

silk handkerchief

top hat

oriental fan

grosgrain bag

walking cane

father's elegant outfit

ostrich-plumed hat

black tailcoat

mother's beautiful party dress

lace collar

striped trousers

dark red velvet

red silk parasol

lace

lace jabot
(put at neck of dress)

house gift—costly vase inside

fragile

rose for mother cat

emeralds

rubies

mother's necklace

Plate 14: **Mother and Father in Party Clothing**

brother's party hat

party snappers

little brother's derby

rosette

Chinese bell

banner

cut out dotted lines in hats

brother's party suit

cane

morning coat

plates

extra balloons

if punch spills, wear other outfit

striped trousers

napkins

green balloon (blow up some more!)

music box

baby's party hat

lemon cake

balloon

party flowers

wind up here

fruit punch

cups

toy bear: Rosebud

put on when baby gets sleepy

hold on to this string

party-favor mints inside

baby's party dress

baby's hat

extra diapers and baby blanket

Plate 15: **Children's Outfits for a Cat Family Party**

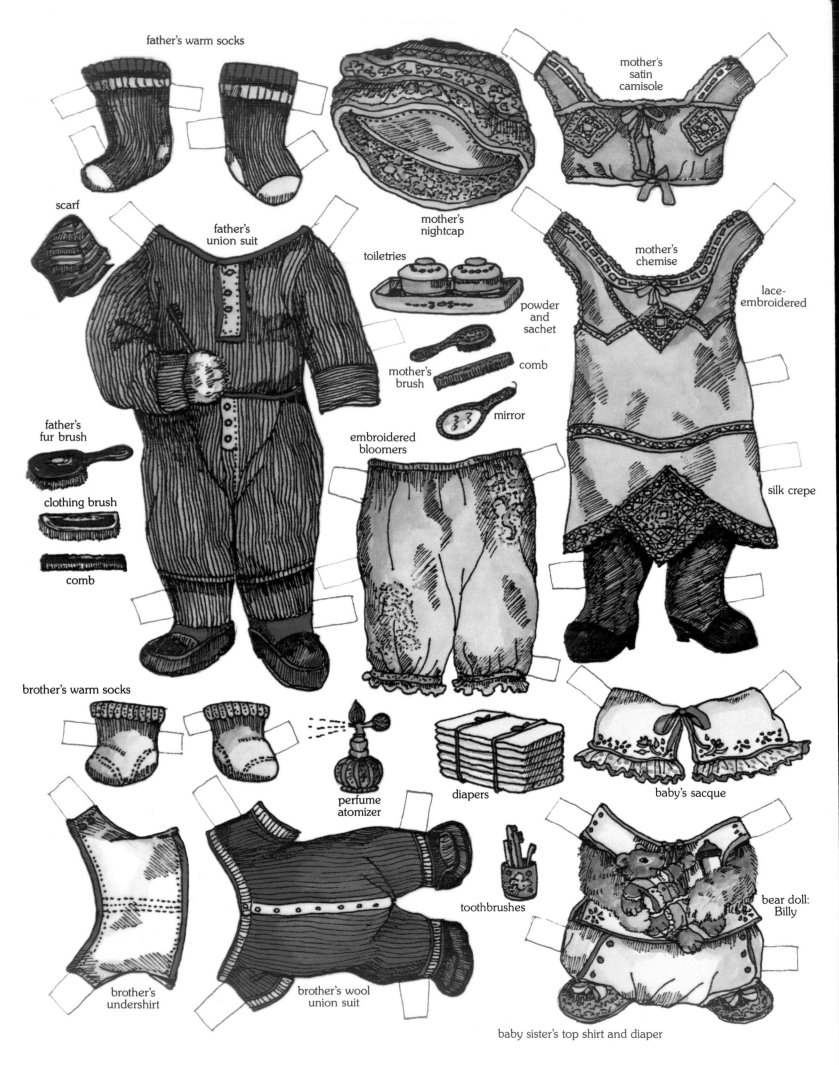

father's warm socks

mother's satin camisole

scarf

father's union suit

mother's nightcap

toiletries

mother's chemise

lace-embroidered

powder and sachet

mother's brush

comb

mirror

father's fur brush

embroidered bloomers

silk crepe

clothing brush

comb

brother's warm socks

perfume atomizer

diapers

baby's sacque

toothbrushes

bear doll: Billy

brother's undershirt

brother's wool union suit

baby sister's top shirt and diaper

Plate 16: The Cat Family's Underclothing and Toiletries